Whazzat?
Closeup Photo Puzzles

Gilbert King

**PUZZLE
WRIGHT
PRESS**

An imprint of Sterling
Publishing Co., Inc.

www.puzzlewright.com

Puzzlewright Press and the distinctive Puzzlewright Press logo
are registered trademarks of Sterling Publishing Co., Inc.

Library of Congress Cataloging-in-Publication Data Available

2 4 6 8 10 9 7 5 3 1

Published by Sterling Publishing Co., Inc.
387 Park Avenue South, New York, NY 10016
© 2011 by Gilbert King
Distributed in Canada by Sterling Publishing
c/o Canadian Manda Group, 165 Dufferin Street
Toronto, Ontario, Canada M6K 3H6
Distributed in the United Kingdom by GMC Distribution Services
Castle Place, 166 High Street, Lewes, East Sussex, England BN7 1XU
Distributed in Australia by Capricorn Link (Australia) Pty. Ltd.
P.O. Box 704, Windsor, NSW 2756, Australia

Printed in China

Sterling ISBN 978-1-4027-7333-4

For information about custom editions, special sales, premium and
corporate purchases, please contact Sterling Special Sales
Department at 800-805-5489 or specialsales@sterlingpublishing.com.

CONTENTS

Introduction

5

Puzzles

7

INTRODUCTION

Everything looks different up close. Details taken out of context can be hard to place, hence the expression "I couldn't see the forest for the trees," although in this book it might be more like "I couldn't see the mouse for the scroll wheel."

On every right-hand page is a picture of a common object, shown from a perspective designed to conceal its identity. If you're stumped, the answer is on the next page—just flip over to reveal a photograph of the same item from a little further away. Or you can always ask for brainstorming help! Just turn to the person sitting next to you and ask, "Whazzat?"

—Gilbert King

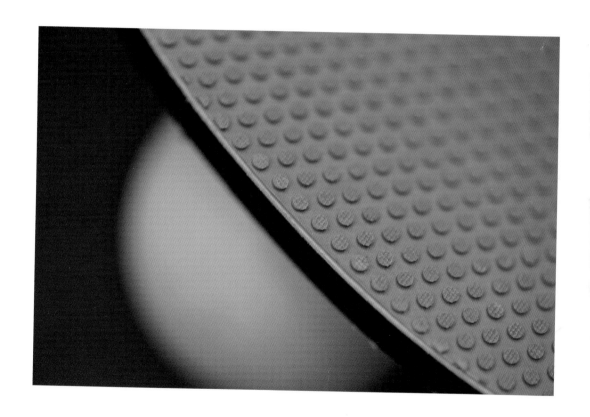

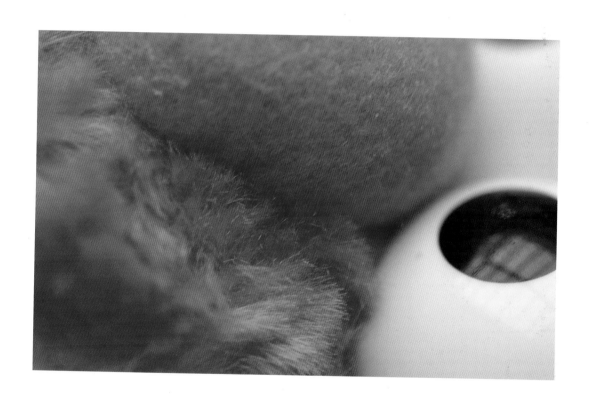

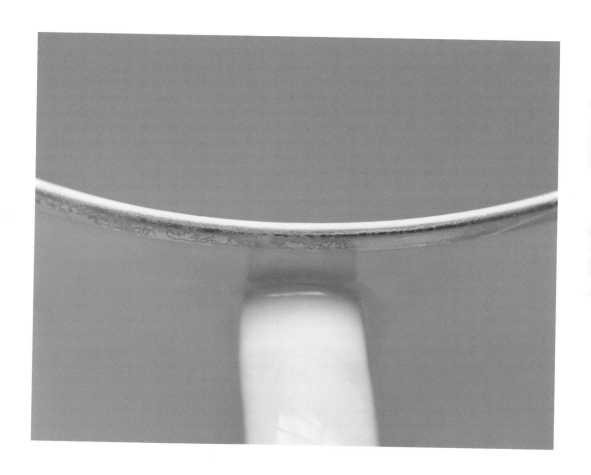

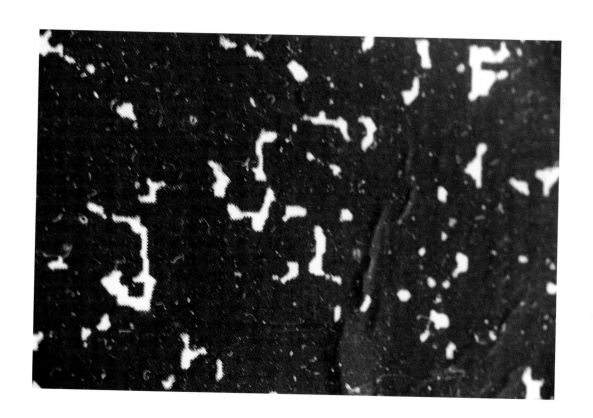

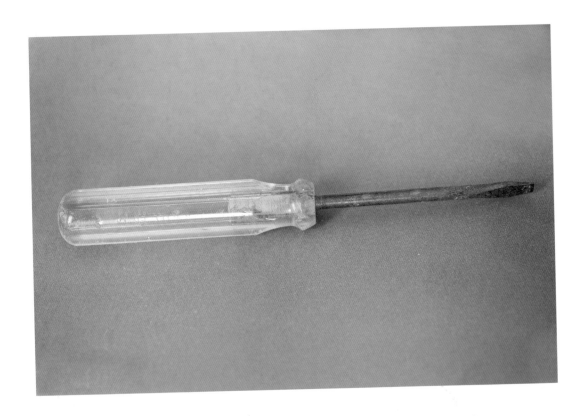

45

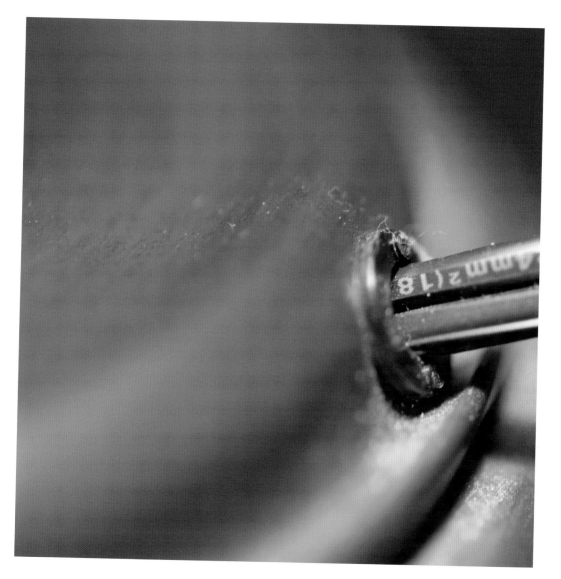

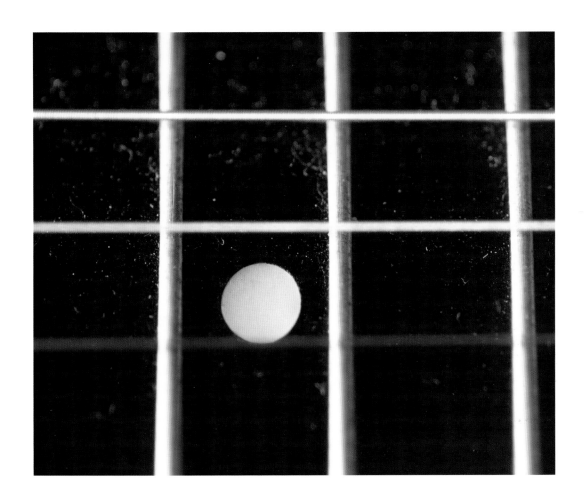

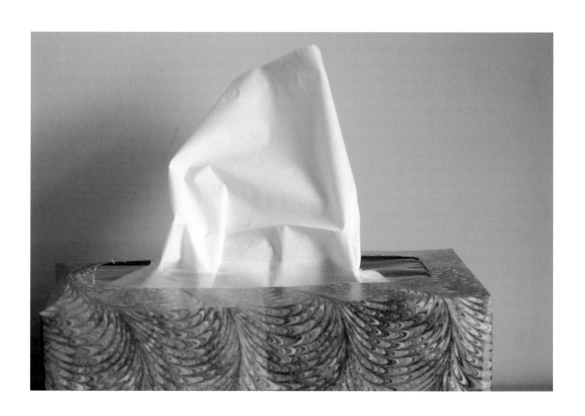

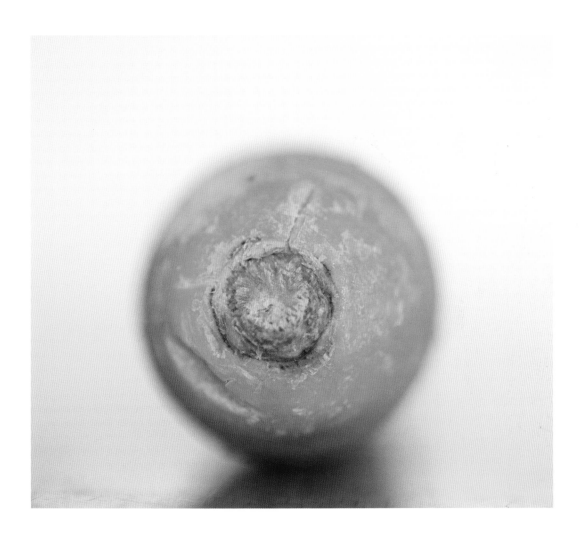

70

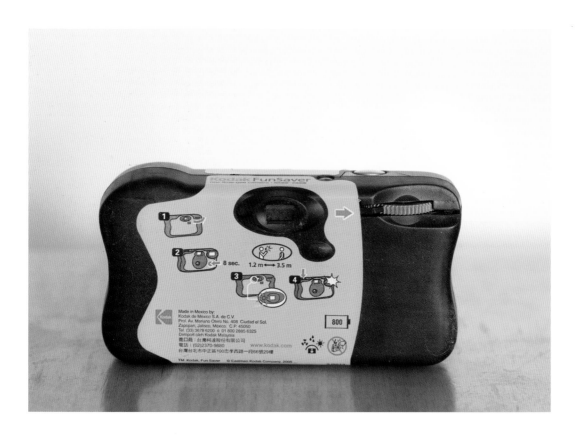

80

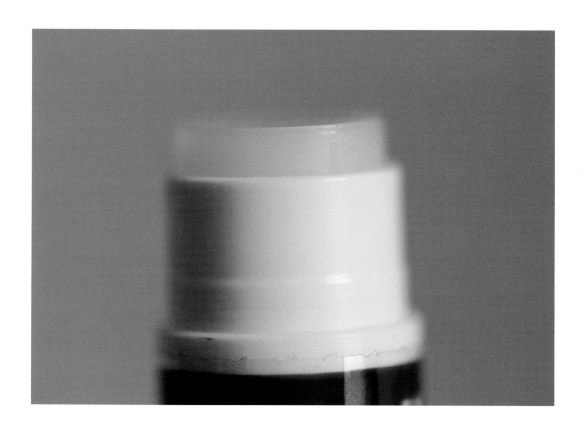

104

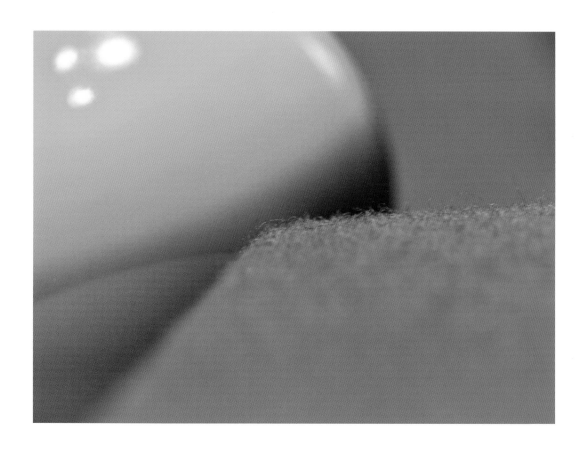

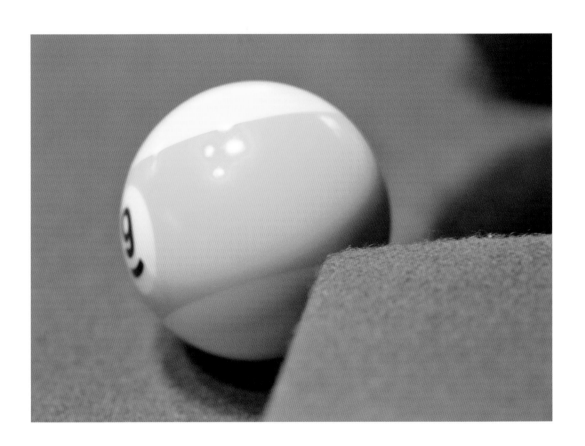

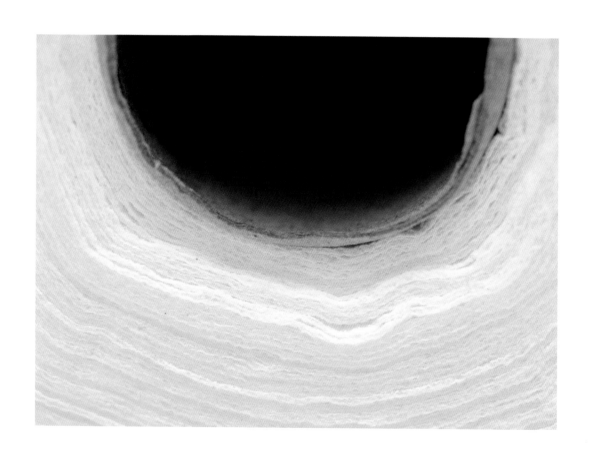

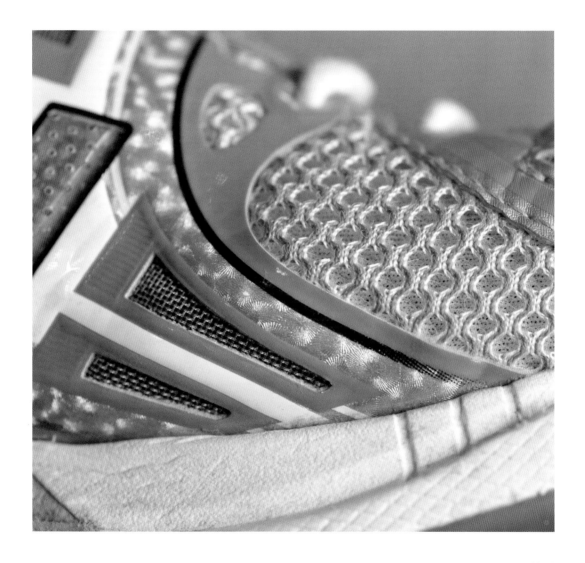

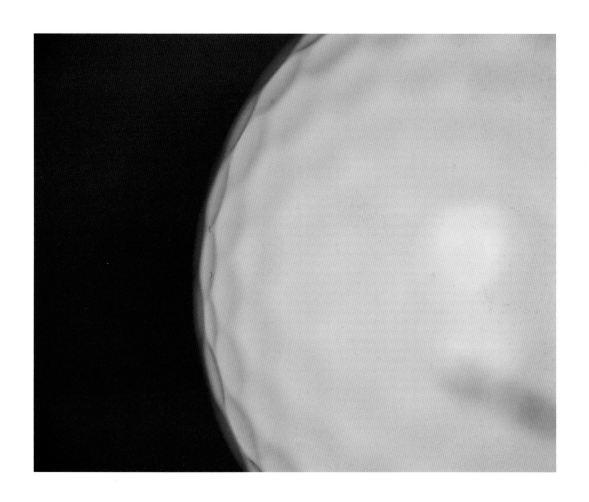

147

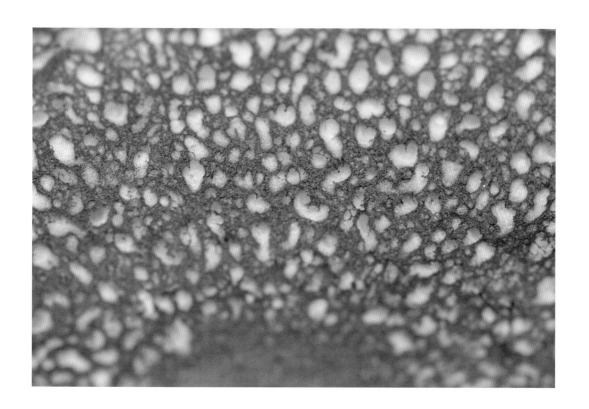

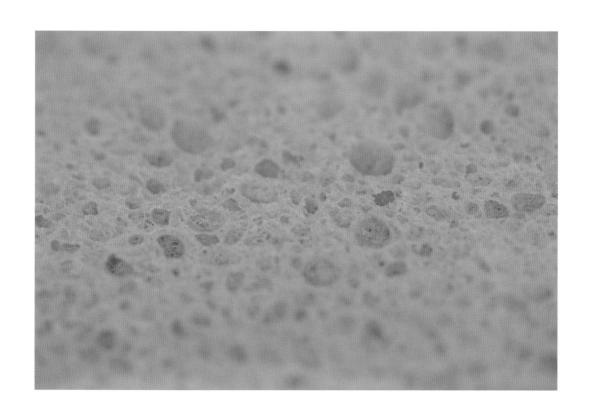

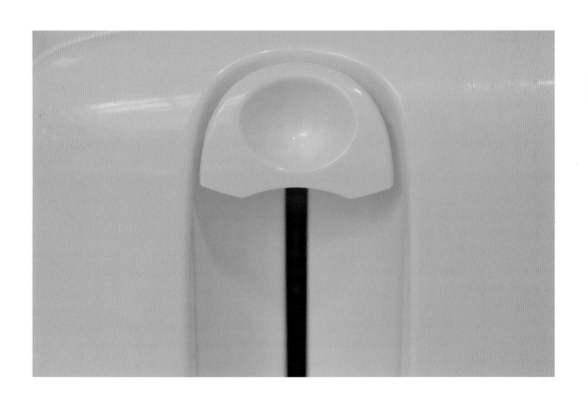

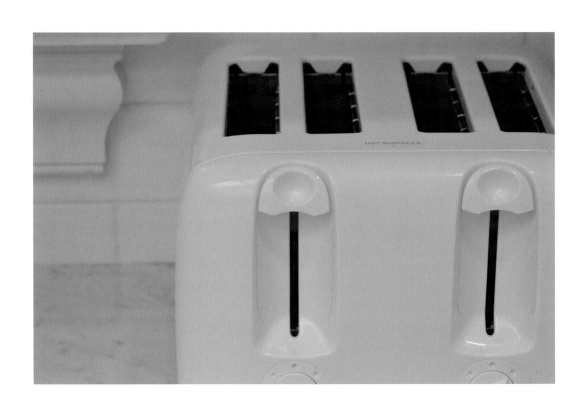

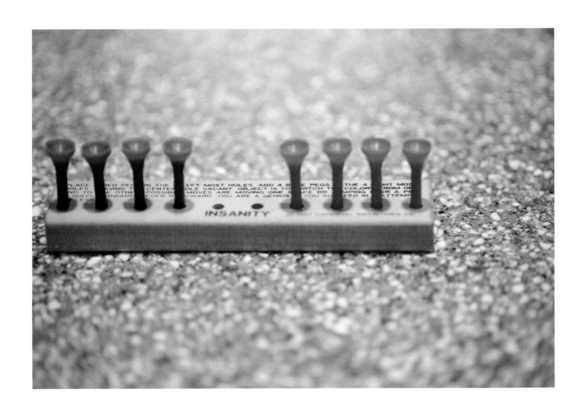

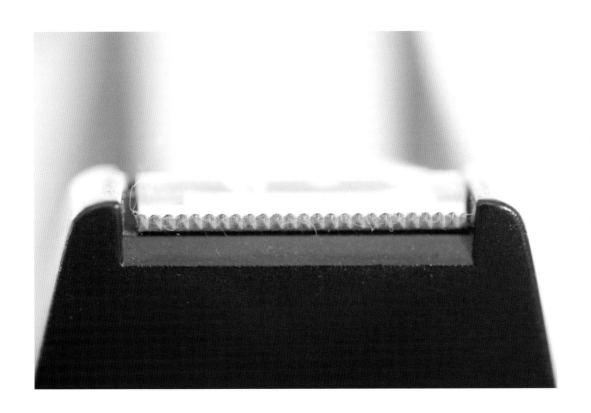

194

198

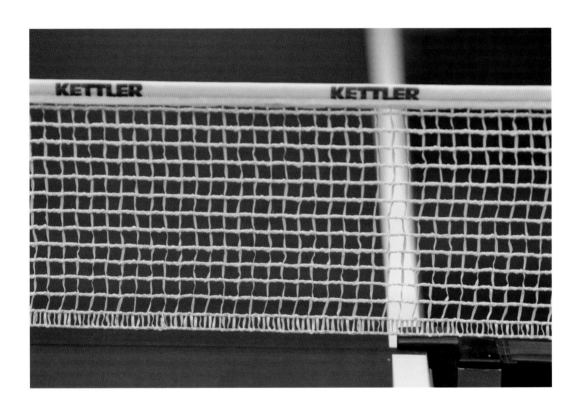

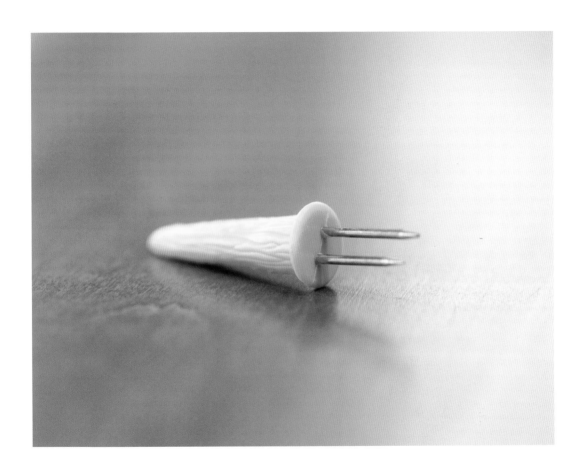

207

210

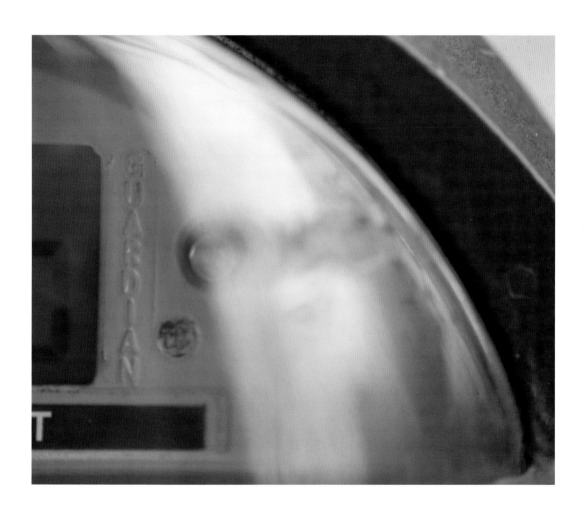

216

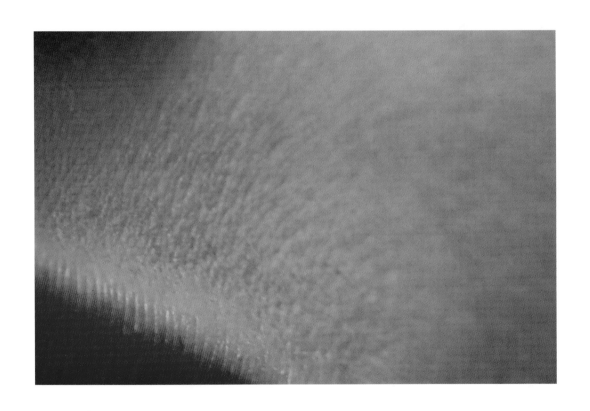

226

230

234

242

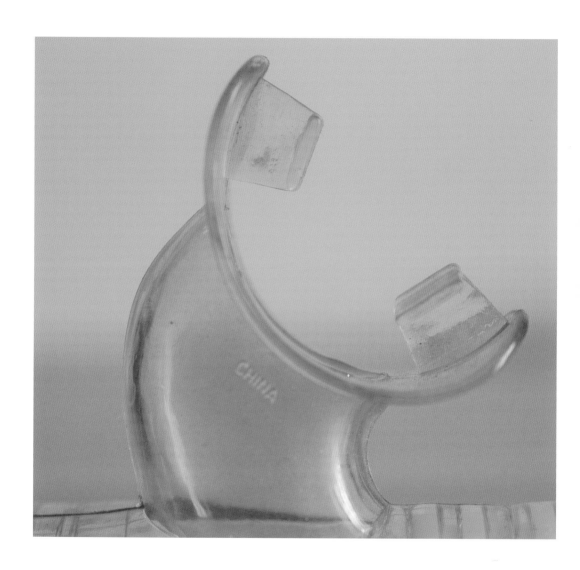

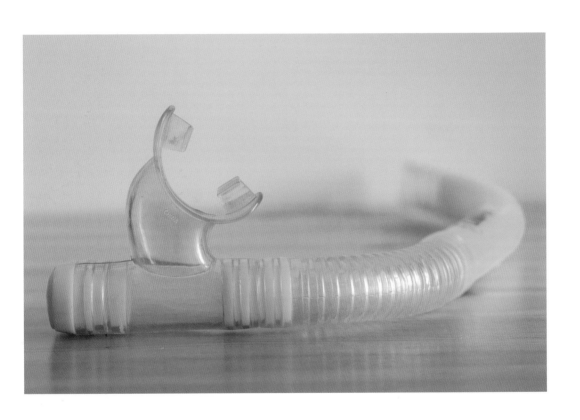

250

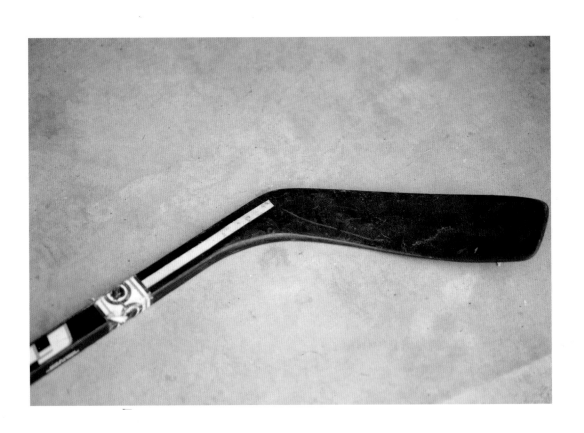

254